A NEW PLATT AMENDMENT

CLIFFORD KENNETH PLATT III

NEWMAN SPRINGS PUBLISHING
320 Broad Street
Red Bank, NJ 07701

First originally published by Newman Springs Publishing 2024

ISBN 979-8-89061-882-5 (Paperback)
ISBN 979-8-89061-883-2 (Digital)

Printed in the United States of America

CONTENTS

To All Patriots…

Where We Go One…We Go All…

AUTHOR'S NOTE

The Platt Amendment of 1901 established the terms under which the United States would end its military occupation of Cuba, that had begun during the Spanish-American War of 1898. This amendment was drafted largely by Secretary of War, Elihu Root, assisted by Senator Orville Platt of Connecticut and was ratified on June 12, 1901 under the administration of President William McKinley. The Platt Amendment would leave control of the island of Cuba to its people, assist the Cuban government in safeguarding its commercial interests, and provide a government capable of maintaining adequate protection of life, property, individual liberty, and Cuban sovereignty.

The Platt Amendment remained in force until 1934, when both countries agreed to cancel the treaties that enforced this amendment, rendering it null and void.

I invite all readers to review the Platt Amendment before reading this book if you have any questions about its outline and directives.

In the writing of this minibook, I plagiarized numerous quotes of our great American ancestors. I do this with the utmost respect for their dedication, bravery, and unconditional service in the formation of our United States of America, which is the hallmark of our country. Our country is at a pivotal point of expansion of its foundation and position in our world that will require the support of all Americans and patriots now to bring the US back on course as a republic once again. A New Platt Amendment could provide the guidance for that new allegiance and alliance of our United States of America.

PREFACE

As I sit and think about writing this book, I ask myself, "Who am I to be writing it?" I remember my history teacher, Mr. Herman, at Massapequa High School in 1968, asking me if the Platt Amendment had any connection with my family. I went home and asked my father at dinner that night. He told me that Senator Orville Platt of Connecticut, one of our relatives, played a role in the drafting of that amendment and that there were other senators in our family lineage as well.

My father, Clifford Kenneth Platt Jr., who served in WWII and Korea, passed on in 2012; and my mother, Ruth Ann Platt, passed on in March 2023. Their ashes were interred in a family plot in Connecticut. Their headstones are a stone's throw from the headstone of another family relative and ancestor, Col. David Hobby, who fought in the American Revolution.

All our family, relatives, and ancestors played an important role in developing the very fabric of our nation that we each take for granted every day. As I get older, I am seeing all of these realities of life much more clearly, like the fact that after WWII ended, my father, Clifford Kenneth Platt Jr., went to military funerals and played taps for the soldier being laid to rest. He confided this to me in his last year of life. He told me that he would go off to a remote part of the cemetery to play taps at the appropriate time during the funeral. I never even knew that he could play the bugle.

Now, as I look back on it all, I find that it all adds up in a whole new way for me in my life, right here, right now.

I am not a writer, although I have been writing since January 17, 2017—strangely, I remember the day.

I am not writing this book because I am a relative of Senator Orville Platt. I am not writing it because of our family history or because I think I am a good writer. I am writing this book because I have to. I have no choice but to write it, however and whatever it becomes. Just as my ancestor Col. David Hobby fought for our new republic, I must, too, with my pen.

America is a land for Americans

This book is a proclamation for all Americans and also for all the people of our world who would, could, or will become an American.

The writing of this book was not a decision that I made. This book came to me in a dream and woke me up with its title. This is not something that I planned or thought about doing. It just happened.

I think that they are all in it together—all my ancestors. Well, I am writing this book now for all of our ancestors, my fellow Americans, and the peoples of this world.

I reviewed the original Platt Amendment and saw the potential it held for how our United States could assist other countries around the world. I could also see its limitations, but it held the basic premise of what A New Platt Amendment could become.

Our world is on a road to perdition and in a time of need for true guidance and leadership. The original Platt Amendment had numerous objectives in its outline, but its overall objective was to establish peace and the ability to maintain it for all parties concerned, and provide stewardship to assist the countries growth and prosperity.

A New Platt Amendment is about our new United States of America becoming a constitutional republic once again and its new leadership role in the world.

A New Platt Amendment is a message for all people, especially Americans, that no matter who or what you are…*we each can live our American Dream, our American way of life.*

A New Platt Amendment—generated to empower, support, and assist all nations that enter this alliance to develop their own constitutional sovereignty—would only support and empower our own constitutional sovereignty.

This book is being written to stoke the fires of patriotism and restore our American United States constitutional republic, along with A New Platt Amendment, that would assist other countries in their quest for life, liberty, and freedom. The world is on the edge in many ways. Each time in American history when our nation was in peril, Americans pulled together and made the grade. Well, now is another time for Americans to *stand up* and *be counted...*

This book is for *everyone*, but especially for those who *stand up, no matter who or where you are...*

INTRODUCTION

A New Platt Amendment is not a discussion, outline, expression, or expansion of the original Platt Amendment in any way, shape, or form.

This book has been written to generate and promote a new, completely free amendment of life, liberty, justice, and free sovereign domain for all countries on this amazing planet.

It is time. Yes, time for humanity to become accountable and responsible to itself and also to the rest of creation and to secure its sovereign freedom now.

Our United States of America has been a corporation since Abraham Lincoln established the United States Reorganization Act of 1871, becoming the first president of this new corporation, ending our republic, and changing our Constitution *for* the United States to a Constitution *of* the United States. This change made our constitution a possession of this corporation and every American a "straw man" liable to the World Federal Reserve Bank of this corporation.

The act, as it was called, provided a municipal government with all its branches to run this foreign-owned corporation known as the United States in the District of Columbia. By the way, the District of Columbia is not a part of the United States of America. Washington DC has become a foreign entity of our American United States.

The Constitution for the United States states that there are only three branches of government—the legislative, judicial, and executive branches—and they must exist on American soil.

The time is long overdue for our United States to return to its constitutional republic and discharge its status as a corporation liable to the monarchy money lenders of the World Federal Reserve Bank, and for our court system to discharge its BAR (British Accreditation Registry).

These monarchs have been cultivating power and control over our world for hundreds of years.

The Constitution for the United States is a proclamation for America and all of humanity.

It is heralding the salvation of our country to become the great nation that our forefathers knew we would eventually become.

Our constitution was written to outline, generate, constitute, and uphold a land of the free and a home of the brave under any and all circumstances.

As long as there are Americans.

A New Platt Amendment would not outline the control and manipulation of a country but support its freedom, empowerment, and constitutional sovereignty as a fellow nation, state, or province of our United States.

Our world is on the threshold of change. For humanity to exist, it must learn to coexist.

This book is an outline of the elements of A New Platt Amendment.

An amendment that will help generate and outline a common decent plan of life for the peoples of each nation to utilize in our quest for planetary stewardship and world peace.

Life is an ever-expanding journey, one that we each must undertake individually, yet it is a journey that we all take together as human beings.

As human beings, we each need to be and become a positive force of creation, one that supports creation and not just the one.

Our illumination shines light for all.

Our light is our freedom…

In this book, I will lay out my perception of what A New Platt Amendment might encompass as its scope, parameter, vision, and quest for our new American republic and new world that is coming forward now.

Creation itself is at the helm of this *lightship*, and *all patriots are called to duty now…*

> A man may die, nations may rise and fall, but an idea lives on. (JFK; January 20, 1961; Presidential Library and Museum)

CONSTITUTIONAL SOVEREIGNTY

*Constitutional. Relating to an established
set of principals governing a state (e.g.,
"a constitutional amendment").*

*Sovereignty. The authority of a state to govern
it-self. supreme power or authority.*

—Oxford Languages

We The People

Our Founding Fathers outlined the principles and mandates of a system of governing ideals for the United States of our new world—a system of governing rules and regulations for a nation in creation under our Creator, upholding creation's light to the best standards of life, liberty, and justice.

United States Declaration of Independence
The Constitution for the United States
United States Bill of Rights

The premise and promise of the documents above are the base and basis of life in our United States and the spirit of our United States here in our nation under our Creator, indivisible, with liberty and justice for all.

The spirit of the people of a nation is the energetic, fortifying factor and the very fabric that upholds that nation.

Our spirit is our strength

The vision of A New Platt Amendment would first and foremost be to uphold the Constitution for our United States everywhere our flag waves.

Our world is mostly water, and as such, maritime law sets the stage in world matters and recognizes each country by its flag. Our flag represents everything to the rest of the world, so to have our flag wave in unison with another country's flag under such an amendment would denote an alliance and allegiance of the United States.

The peoples of the world love America and what it stands for. Thus, for a nation, state, or province to desire an agreement with the United States would make that land a united state with the United States of America, no matter where they are.

The world will not fit in the United States, but the world can be a part of the United States. This way, the peoples of the world can develop their own American Dream.

Our world is a macrocosm and a microcosm at the same time. Every aspect of creation is surfacing to be expressed now, and the all of the all of creation is revealing itself to the world.

> Macrocosm. The whole of a complex structure especially the world or universe.

> Microcosm. A community, place or situation regarded as encapsulating in miniature the characteristics, qualities, or features of some-thing much larger.

Now is the time, more than ever, for our world to assemble itself and unite under the articles of common decency and rights of life to uphold our Creator's light on this beautiful planet and continue our journey from darkness. New energies of creation in our New Age of Aquarius are driving our world forward into the light.

Yes, forward out of the limitations that have held humanity and all of creation in check politically, religiously, physically, and mentally worldwide. People all around the globe are beginning to see, feel, know, and understand these realities that the Constitution for the United States denotes, promotes, and upholds as our doctrine of freedom and, even more than that, our way of life. They all want to come here and have this reality become their reality of life. As I said before, our United States is only so big. The world will not fit in the United States, but the United States will fit in the world.

Our forefathers, who came to America, came to establish a new world free of the limitations of life, liberty, and justice for all. Our nation has been built on these realities of life outlined in our constitution.

In 1823, President James Monroe established the Monroe Doctrine, a principle of the US policy that states that any intervention by external powers in the politics of the Americas is a potentially hostile act against the US. A New Platt Amendment would provide a broader outline for clearer, more precise boundaries for world governments.

The United States is waking up once again to the reality that the world and the US are transitioning now energetically. All people everywhere are expressing their new realities of life. Now, even more than ever, the constitution needs to be upheld and reinforced with the energies of life, liberty, and justice for all.

The peoples of this world have looked to the US as a role model ever since we became a nation. Our world is in dire straits right now in so many ways. We cannot fix the problems of the world, but if we can uphold our constitution and bring our nation back on course as a republic, then we will have accomplished so much more than just becoming the greatest nation in the world once again. We will also be a nation that will inspire our world.

A New Platt Amendment would uphold constitutional sovereignty for every country in the world that chooses to join the United States Republic for America in an alliance. All nations entering an alliance with the US would still be their own nation with complete sovereignty yet agree to uphold the Constitution for the United States within the confines of their specific nation and also in their diplomatic relations worldwide. Their country would become its own version of the US and develop its own special specific realities of life, liberty, and justice for all.

It is time for the United States to harness its constitutional sovereignty as a republic once again. We the people must band together as Americans and stand firm as one nation under God, indivisible, with liberty and justice for all.

We the people have the right.
We the people have the light.
We the people have the power.

The energies of creation are supporting all Americans and all people everywhere to become sovereign in their own lives now. Freedom and free sovereign domain for every American will be a unilateral reality of life as long as we regenerate our constitutional republic. We have the right, the light, and the power of creation and our Creator supporting every one of us on our journey of life.

We each are empowered with these inalienable rights that we each should hold as our personal reality of life to be empowered individually yet work together collectively as units of unity.

Constitutional sovereignty is our birthright. This truth and reality were first put in writing as the Magna Carta on June 15, 1215, proclaiming that the king and his government were not above the law. It is time for the world to wake up to this fact and live this reality now.

A New Platt Amendment will support and uphold our constitutional sovereignty and sovereign way of life in America worldwide for all people to utilize as their way of life. As the United States becomes re-empowered constitutionally as a republic, it will take its place once again as the greatest nation in the world. All people worldwide will look toward America for their guidance and empowerment personally, professionally, and politically.

I am not proposing that the United States should rule the world. I am proposing that the United States get its house in order as a constitutional republic, reorganize and rebuild our country, and generate A New Platt Amendment that will assist other nations around the world to do the same, making everything great again.

The United States is not about being the best country in the world. It is about being the best that we can be because that is how humanity was designed by our Creator to become.

Our freedom is calling to every one of us right now. We the people need to decide who we are going to be. Everything that has taken place in our world is bringing us to this new chapter of America's new sovereign republic, along with the discharge of its corporation, world bank, and bar.

Let our three cannons roar.

Yes, roar for their discharge.

A New Platt Amendment will outline this new freedom for all united states of our new American republic as one nation under God, indivisible, with liberty and justice for all.

UNABRIDGED FREEDOM

Unabridged. Not cut or shortened; complete.

Freedom. The power or right to act, think,
or speak as one wants without hindrance
or restraint; absence of subjection to foreign
domination or despotic government; the
state of not being imprisoned or enslaved.

Our world is coalescing its personal power of freedom now. The masses globally are invoking their rights and demanding that their governments support them and shift with them to a more balanced, harmonious way of life. The implementation of authoritarian systems of power and control are being vanquished worldwide now as we the people wake up to these archaic principles being promoted now by the global elite in control worldwide.

Freedom and free domain are the order of the day now

A New Platt Amendment could become an outline and layout for all countries to utilize as their design for their own American Dream. This amendment would uphold its primary objective of freedom at the forefront and heart of its main directive, providing a clear and level playing field for all countries to form an alliance that supports a unified world.

We are entering the House of Aquarius in the zodiac once again. While many do not pay attention to these realities, nonetheless, they are real and have a great effect energetically on our world and humanity itself.

Aquarian principles and values are all about freedom, rebirth, and renewal, with a strong desire for innovative change collectively. Humanity will naturally develop an overwhelming capacity and ability for new humanitarian concepts and outlines of our new ways of life coming forth now.

Our world is moving past and beyond its antiquated systems of power and control. These systems served creation for hundreds of years, but they are outdated now and only limit the expansion of our Creator's kingdom of light, the children of creation, and our planet.

Unabridged freedom is the new reality of life coming forward for all people everywhere now.

Nothing can stop this reality from being generated now. Our world is expanding its parameters of light; and along with this new light and illumination will be higher levels of wisdom, love, and grace.

We are talking about an all-new society of creation, from free limitless energy to the wisdom of the ages in new technologies beyond comprehension, like flying hydrogen, cold fusion electromagnetic automobiles that will set our world on a new course of freedom from so many limiting realities of life that can no longer be upheld.

We as a people, planet, and universe are moving up once again from the industrial age of Pisces creation into the spiritual age of Aquarian adventure.

As the frequencies of creation expand, so do the technologies. Humanity must now become accountable unto itself, the world, and all the new freedoms coming forward now to creation.

A New Platt Amendment would have parameters and outlines of creative capacity, energy utilization, and planetary stewardship that all nations in alliance would honor.

While we all will have the freedom of the ages at our fingertips in a whole new way, this freedom will also now come with responsibility and accountability for our freedom.

Our new world will have very clear, clean, precise directives of life for all people everywhere to honor along with their freedom.

You might say that this does not sound like true freedom, but all realities of life in creation come with their own responsibilities that we each must be accountable for. So in our new unabridged freedom, we each will have that complete freedom but also have to be responsible for that freedom.

We are all looking at a whole, completely new way of life from the ground up. It will be excitingly, exhilaratingly adventurous with all the freedoms it will hold; yet at the same time, it will take time to develop as our new way of life. This is where A New Platt Amendment would be a game changer to assist all nations to be able to hold their balance in the face of extreme new realities of creation and of life.

Just think of a world that is no longer tied to the wheel or the power grid any longer!

Just these two new realities of creation will change our world dramatically. People would be able to live in many more areas of our planet that were considered uninhabitable before.

Our world is waking up to many new freedoms of life presenting themselves to humanity now. People everywhere are expressing many new forms of freedom that they are declaring as their new freedoms. They desire a world that supports these new freedoms as a way of life that everyone should accept.

A New Platt Amendment would have a constitutional outline of the basic freedoms that each member would use as their guideline for universal applications of alliance supporting all basic rights generated by our Creator and creation itself.

Our rights of freedom apply to all of creation now. Each new form of freedom would only be acceptable if it did not invade the freedom of another and also did not generate limitations of life, liberty, or the pursuit of happiness.

Our United States constitution provides very clear parameters of unabridged freedom that would be the best outline for a world system of united states, provinces, nations, and countries to organize under A New Platt Amendment.

Just as our country owes its greatness to our constitution, so could other nations enter into an alliance under its provisions too as our world begins our new Aquarian adventure together, *unabridged…*

UNILATERAL EXPRESSION

*Unilateral. An action or decision affecting
one person or country involved in a particular
situation without the agreement of another or the
others (e.g., "universal nuclear disarmament").*

*Expression. The process of making
known one's thoughts or feelings.*

There is a unilateral expression of solidarity throughout the world now. It comes forth in many ways, through many different groups of people, in many places around the world, and through individual unilateral expressions of sovereignty.

Solidarity. Unity or agreement of feeling or action especially among individuals with a common interest; mutual support within a group.

The difference now is that this worldwide solidarity is in direct confrontation with the political regimes that currently rule the world and are trying to implement their new world order of complete power and control worldwide. Our world is shifting to a new level of enlightenment and consciousness now.

For the United States of America to become a great nation once again, it would then have to be and become a world leader and provide A New Platt Amendment for other nations to utilize for their empowerment if they needed guidance and assistance on their road forward to becoming their own great nation.

We are dealing with our world now, and yes, there will be a new world order, but not one of power and control. Our new world order will be of brotherhood and unity among nations working together. This is how we will all tackle the problems of our world and generate a peaceful, harmonious, tranquil, abundant, clean, pristine world for all of humanity.

A New Platt Amendment would outline unilateral procedures of creation and destruction of matter, generating a pristine new world and eliminating waste and pollution.

We have the wisdom, knowledge, and power to make this a reality worldwide now.

The idea of controlling another nation for its specific attributes is not the answer; it is the problem. Unilateral expression is the order of the day now. Unilateral expression brings responsibility and accountability to the forefront of life now as a way of life—period.

It is time for all people worldwide to decide what kind of world we will create: a world of pollution, death, and destruction, or a world filled with peace, harmony, alliance, and life. Our wars are no longer the devastating destruction of WWII; now they are nuclear.

Our Constitution for the United States was written by men who, in their time of need, became Americans and generated the Constitution for the United States to uphold their new world. In their day, this was their unilateral expression.

The world is hungry now for this reality to come forth for humanity.

We are talking about so much more than America and our United States now. Sure, we can pull our nation back together, but how long will that last if the rest of the world exists in chaos?

Humanity is at the crossroads of shifting from the power and control of humanity to an alliance of humanity in a humane unilateral expression of humanitarian values for world peace and the preservation of the sanctity of life and our world.

> Humane. Having or showing compassion or benevolence.

> Humanitarian. Concerned with or seeking to promote the welfare and sanctity of life.

> Sanctity. The state or quality of being holy, sacred, or saintly.

I am painting a picture here for the United States and for the whole world. I am painting it for humanity to take heart, take heed, and take action toward freedom, equality, and justice for all people worldwide, not just Americans.

This book will not be very long. I am not looking to write the outline of A New Platt Amendment in it now. I see this book as an idea, a dream, a vision, and a quest for this book to plant a seed that will sprout and grow worldwide, like a match that ignites a fire shining a light that all can see or *a shot heard around the world* (1775).

A New Platt Amendment, in its full scope and outline, will be a work of art much broader than this book. This book is just the idea and the seed sprouting straight to the point for all the people of this beautiful world to grasp and take hold of now.

The Age of Aquarius is here. It will last for two thousand years. The illumination of this new world it is bringing has begun. Nothing can stop this awakening and new reality of life.

It is just a matter of time…

WORLD INDEPENDENCE

*World. The Earth together with all of its
countries, peoples, and natural features.*

*Independence. The fact or state
of being independent.*

All the people on this beautiful planet are in a state of transition now. This is a time in creation where our planet leaves one house of the zodiac and enters another, generating the beginning of a new cycle of creation. We are leaving the house of Pisces and entering the house of Aquarius.

I make this statement again because I wish everyone to realize and understand that all the turmoil going on worldwide is in direct relation to this reality and also to other major reality changes taking place now. This book is not about those changes; it is about where we are going with these changes as a people and as a planet.

These new realities of creation being revealed to humanity now are nothing new; in fact, the revelations being revealed now are ancient and have been hidden for a long time.

I am not here to discuss these realities either. What I am here to outline is the fact that we as a people and planet have the ability to break away from all limiting controls now and generate our free domain, our freedom.

We each are being given by our creator the wisdom, love, and grace to shift beyond these limitations toward our freedom. These limitations that I speak of come from a system of governing aristocracies that have been in power and control of our world for hundreds of years.

> Aristocracy. The highest class in certain societies, especially those holding hereditary titles or offices.

These rulers have provided their form of power and control for generations of time. Now is the time for humanity to generate our true freedom with governments that are of the people, by the people, and for the people worldwide, represented by A New Platt Amendment under our constitutional sovereignty and power of creation as human beings and the children of our Creator.

For world independence to ever become a true reality, our world needs to generate a provincial agreement or treaty of alliance and conduct for the nations of our world to adhere to in an open, honest, dignified manner.

A New Platt Amendment would not only empower and support all nations or countries that chose to form an alliance; it would also provide parameters of creation as an outline for the world to consider as a step toward true alliance and brotherhood, supporting progressive, positive outlines for the creation and recycling of all the different product materials that humanity utilizes, generating a balanced ecosystem worldwide.

Science and technology are moving into uncharted waters beyond comprehension. Our governments are outlining our mandates of creation above and beyond normal parameters of life, liberty, and the pursuit of happiness.

It is time for accountability and responsibility worldwide.

We—as in every one of us—must now become accountable and responsible for ourselves on every level of life. A New Platt

Amendment would help all nations support one another and build a world of positive cohesion that supports individual empowerment, accountability, and responsibility collectively worldwide.

We the people hold the keys to the kingdom. Our Creator has given every human being a heart and a soul. We each have these rights of creation running through our veins.

Together we stand, divided we fall. It is obvious now which road we each must travel. In unity, there is strength, power, and freedom.

World independence will be a huge game changer. For our world to be truly independent, there would be no wars, and peace would prevail worldwide.

We will need all the help that we can get to achieve this reality of life. A New Platt Amendment would help organize, outline, and mandate the parameters of such an adventure.

ESSENTIAL DIRECTIVES

Essential. Absolutely necessary;
extremely important.

Directive. An official or authoritative
instruction involving the management
or guidance of operations.

Life on our planet has run amok with corporate power and control advancing forth like a Trojan army with many new forms of their horse.

Like the game Monopoly that we have all played, eventually one player owns the board, and the other player becomes a slave to the board.

This is okay for a game; but in real life, it spells war, destruction, and death eventually, as life becomes unbearable for the 99 percent.

The time is now. Yes, time for essential directives of creation.

A New Platt Amendment would outline these essential directives of creation for all partnering countries, provinces, and nations to utilize as common, decent, proficient outlines of life and of creation for the benefit of that country and the entire world.

Our world is advancing scientifically beyond imagination, and there are beings that are utilizing this technology to enslave and eliminate all that stands in their way. After WWII, the Nuremberg trials provided some accountability for the atrocities that were committed.

A New Platt Amendment would need to be orchestrated with a complete outline of essential directives for the *generation* and *destruction* of all matter in our new world to uphold the life, liberty, freedom, and pursuit of happiness of all human beings worldwide.

Just as our world leaders negotiate nuclear treaties, there now needs to be biological and technological treaties that outline the generation and destruction of creation.

There needs to be clear provisions of creation and destruction in all the arenas of life now to maintain our beautiful world and not turn it into a scientific or technological experiment.

There are codes of conduct for all avenues of creation that must be outlined and upheld. The human genome was not designed to become a machine or be chemically reorganized into a new form of life.

There are very serious situations of creation that exist on our planet right now that threaten our very fabric of life, along with governments that are out of control and need to be brought back into balance.

The United States has been a world leader for over two hundred years, and the Constitution for the United States is the best essential directive ever created.

Now, under A New Platt Amendment, our constitution could be expanded to outline essential directives of our new realities of life being generated throughout our world to maintain our base and basis of life, liberty, and the pursuit of happiness.

For all of humanity.

ORGANIC REPUBLIC

Organic. Relating to or derived from living matter; produced without the use of artificial agents.

Republic. A state in which supreme power is held by the people and their elected representatives, and which has an elected or nominated president rather than a monarch.

Human beings are genetically organic by nature. We each hold this reality as our fundamental base of life in our United States as one nation under God, indivisible, with liberty and justice for all.

No matter how much AI wants to turn all people into robots, we are human beings with a heart and a soul. Eternal life does not come in a can. It comes from our heart and soul...

We as a people organically generated this nation with our hearts and souls, literally. Our forefathers, our ancestors put forth the "Constitution for the United States" for our country forever, and for everyone who wished to become an American.

I think about my ancestor Col. David Hobby, who fought in the American Revolution, and what those early Americans went through in their struggle to build a new world out of the wilderness and break free of the tyrannical powers that drove them to this new land.

My whole life and this book came forward to me as my new personal truth and reality that I must acknowledge. The culmination of about 69 years of life all of a sudden adding up in a whole new way. Like a painting that you just finished and now you can see the picture clearly.

Oh my God…

Well, we all have our organic ancestors, or we would not be here. Yes, the people who forged this world and cast creation for future generations to come.

This is why our Constitution begins with "We The People."

"We The People" are all a race of human beings on one Earth under our Creator…

Our world can be and become an Organic Republic, if that is what we choose.

So I say again, our United States was forged by all of our ancestors who came to this new world and created it. Now "We The People" can follow this plan of life and expand it through "A New Platt Amendment" to encompass our world as United States and United Countries.

You can call it whatever you like just as long as "We The People" find a way to get our United States back on track along with the rest of the world.

We are our Creator's children. What are we going to create with what we have been given?

In an Organic Republic, there would be no government or corporate monopoly monarchs controlling the major institutions of a free world.

They have done their job well. They have awakened many sleeping giants. Those that choose their road, so be it. But as for the rest of humanity, we need "A New Platt Amendment" right here, right now.

We are the ancestors of tomorrow's world. It is time for all Americans, all patriots, and all peoples of this world who choose to step forth into the light of our new world to stand up and be counted…

Our Organic Republic will be forged by "We The People," taking back our country, taking back our world. It is not theirs. It is ours, "We The People," and this is our call to action…

Take heart, take heed, and take hold of your life now. Band together with your brothers and sisters and confirm our Declaration of Independence, Constitution, and Bill of Rights to be our true forum of life, liberty, and justice for all United States of an American Republic.

Our world is expanding in so many new ways right now, not in the future. Now is the time to begin to generate an outline and layout for this new world.

"A New Platt Amendment" could be the plan that gives the world its aperture, outline, guidance, vision, and quest for the proper generation of a world alliance that supports all of humanity and our beautiful planet for generations and centuries to come.

Don't tread on US (Patrick Henry; 1776–2024).

CONCLUSION

I have learned a lot from writing this little book. It is meant to be short and to the point so that all people can understand the reality and importance of this information easily and clearly without a lot of banter. When I write a book, the idea of the project comes to me first; and then as I write the book, it all comes forth from me.

What I am sharing here is the fact that we the people may not know what we are going to do about bringing back our United States to a republic and generating A New Platt Amendment, but if we just decide to do it, then at least we have made the commitment and started our journey.

We are *we the people*; this is our home, our land, and our world. We have an obligation to maintain them. The great liberties by which we live have been fought for numerous times. It is our right, our duty, and our responsibility to make sure that we get the kind of leadership that maintains our republic and government, of the people, by the people, and *for the people*.

What is it they say? The journey of a thousand miles begins with the first step. Well, let's all just make that first step and look for the next step.

So take that first step, look around, and see what might be the next. Maybe it is just telling the first person you see after you take that first step about what you are doing and how you feel about all of this.

Grassroots campaigns start small, one blade of grass at a time. But it does not take long before you have a field of dreams.

We are the people, yes, plain and simple. We all want to live our lives, and enjoy our family, friends, and world.

We have the ability to create any kind of world that we would like now if we can unite and live together.

Why not take the time now to at least try? Time to take that first step and begin our journey to our new field of dreams.

In my Monopoly game, our world is filled with organic republics that are constitutionally sovereign and free and coexist in harmonious peace.

This book is about regenerating our American republic and sovereign way of life.

It has been generated to plant seeds of faith, hope, love, and grace in our world for all human beings to come together and unify in the common interest of life, liberty, and the pursuit of happiness for everyone.

This starts with every one of us, right here and right now. It can be as simple as just changing the way that you interact and treat people in your life, expressing your truth responsibly, and being accountable for your thoughts, words, deeds, and actions honestly.

Taking the time to be an American is what made America great. It is what will make America great again. Make everything great again. MAGA-MEGA.

A New Platt Amendment would be a way for this reality to become our reality worldwide.

> Ask not what your country can do for you, but
> what you can do for your country. (JFK; January
> 20, 1961)

ABOUT THE AUTHOR

Clifford Kenneth Platt III a.k.a. Clif LaPlant is a writer and energy consultant whose books express his inner visions and feelings of creation for humanity as our world shifts forth into its new Age of Aquarius. He presents many unique, positive, possible realities of life for humanity to consider.

His desire is that everyone reading his books will find new levels of their own wisdom, power, love, and grace within themselves on our sovereign journey of life together…